faith first

Legacy Edition

Activities and Assessment Tools

A Blackline Master Book
with Answer Keys

Morality

Anne Battes-Kirby
Tina DeCamp
Judy Deckers

RESOURCES FOR CHRISTIAN LIVING®

www.FaithFirst.com

NIHIL OBSTAT
Rev. Msgr. Robert M. Coerver
Censor Librorum
IMPRIMATUR
† Most Rev. Charles V. Grahmann
Bishop of Dallas

August 8, 2005

Send all inquiries to:
RCL • Resources for Christian Living
200 East Bethany Drive
Allen, Texas 75002-3804

Toll Free   877-275-4725
Fax   800-688-8356

Visit us at **www.rclweb.com**
              www.FaithFirst.com

Printed in the United States of America

20513   ISBN 0-7829-1102-1

1 2 3 4 5 6 7 8 9 10
05 06 07 08 09 10 11

Contents

About This Book

Growing as a person of faith involves looking at the world and at our actions in a new, faith-filled way. Seeing our lives through the prism of faith transforms everything. The *Faith First Legacy Edition Activities and Assessment Tools* booklets will help young people polish that prism in enriching ways.

Structure

This booklet is divided into two sections. In the first section you will find twenty four activities—two for each of the twelve chapters in the student book. In the second section you will find a two-page chapter test for each of the twelve chapters as well as two four-page unit assessments. There is an answer key provided at the end of each section.

A Comprehensive Tool

When these activities and tests are added to the wealth of support material in the catechist and teacher guides and on **FaithFirst.com**, you have a comprehensive group of tools to help the young people in your care have an enriching experience as they grow in faith this year.

Remember: Every page in this booklet is perforated for easy tear-out and the entire booklet is reproducible.

God bless you in your important work, and have a great year using *Faith First Legacy Edition*.

Activities

Introduction to Activities

The additional activities in this booklet for *Faith First Legacy Edition* have two principal values. They give young people an opportunity to analyze and synthesize the new faith knowledge they are gaining and to express their learning in a variety of ways.

The Table of Contents includes the corresponding chapter number and title and booklet page number for each activity. Each activity page is clearly marked at the top with the chapter number and title. The footer on the bottom right contains the student book title. This will be helpful if you or the students are filing the activities and you use more than one *Faith First Legacy* junior high booklet during the year.

Activity Features

Each activity includes clear directions and ample space for completion. For activities that suggest the design of a poster or collage, you may wish to offer the young people poster board or art paper to complete the activity. Almost all the activities can be completed by a student working independently. However, some students do their best work when working with a group, so consider letting them do so from time to time. There is a "Faith Action" suggested on the bottom of each activity page to help the young people carry the activity theme out in their lives. You may wish to have them record their responses to the "Faith Action" suggestions in faith journals they may be keeping.

Kinds of Activities

You'll find that the activities throughout Faith First Legacy Edition appeal to a variety of styles of learning and ways of expressing learning. This variety allows students to express themselves verbally, visually, and kinesthetically. They will have the chance to use their intelligence and their imagination to extend their learning by applying faith knowledge to new situations and possibilities.

Portfolios

Invite the young people to include their best work on these activities in their portfolios if they are compiling them. The use of portfolios in religious education is discussed in more detail in the Assessment section on page 44.

Answer Key for Activities

There is a complete Answer Key for Activities beginning on page 31. It includes solution diagrams for all word puzzles and suggestions for appropriate responses where student responses might vary but should allude to certain faith content.

The Way to Happiness: A Word Search

As we study Catholic morality it is important to remember that we are all treasured children of God. The path we choose to happiness should be guided by the principles of Catholic morality. To help you remember the central message of this chapter, figure out what words in the puzzle the clues represent. Then find the word in the grid. Words can go horizontally, vertically, and diagonally in all eight directions.

Clues

❖ The grace that empowers us to live as God's adopted sons and daughters

❖ Describe the way to happiness

❖ The ability to choose to make God the center of our lives

❖ Living our life in Christ

❖ The power to know God

❖ A spiritual journey

❖ The grace that makes us holy or one with God

❖ The spiritual and immortal part of the human person

L	Z	S	E	D	U	T	I	T	A	E	B
S	A	N	C	T	I	F	Y	I	N	G	T
M	G	G	R	C	G	J	W	B	P	M	L
R	M	L	N	H	P	L	B	I	M	A	T
F	B	H	Y	D	K	R	L	C	U	L	C
D	R	P	O	Q	D	G	M	T	V	R	E
Z	F	E	R	L	R	R	C	J	V	M	L
C	H	M	E	I	I	A	Y	W	S	J	L
Y	L	V	M	W	N	N	K	P	O	C	E
V	L	A	G	T	I	B	E	Q	U	N	T
Z	G	B	H	P	X	L	Z	S	L	L	N
E	T	D	G	B	L	D	L	X	S	H	I

Faith Action

Write a sentence describing true happiness. Carry it with you this week and refer to it as you are making choices. Before you act determine whether your choice will contribute to true happiness or not.

My Blueprint for Happiness

In the Sermon on the Mount, Jesus gave us the blueprint for happiness—the Beatitudes. If we live the Beatitudes and make wise decisions, we will find our way to true happiness—being blessed by God now and forever in heaven. Think about decisions you make every day that affect the happiness of your family, friends, neighbors, and yourself. Then work with a partner and create a blueprint for happiness by completing the phrases below.

Family happiness is _____.

I can help by _____.

Friendship happiness is _____.

I can help by _____.

Neighborhood happiness is _____.

I can help by _____.

My happiness is _____.

I can _____.

 Faith Action

Make a commitment to do one thing this week to contribute to the true happiness of someone in your family.

Four Square Vocabulary: Disciple

Chapter 2 examines the dilemma of a wealthy young man in the Gospel of Mark. His dilemma rested in his decision whether to be a disciple of Christ. Using your textbook, define the word *disciple* in the four squares.

1. Define the term using the textbook definition.

2. Define the term using your own words.

3. Use the term in a sentence.

4. Draw a picture to define the term.

Faith Action

At the end of each day this week, think back over the wise decisions you made—both large and small. Say a short prayer thanking God for the wisdom to make these decisions.

Making Decisions: A Short Play

Each day you are faced with making decisions to follow Jesus. These decisions affect the way you choose to live your life. In Chapter 2 you are learning about the decision the wealthy young man was faced with making. Take a minute to reflect on and then discuss the questions in the box with a partner. Work with the same partner to plan a skit that portrays young people who resolve a moral dilemma by using a wise decision-making process.

Discussion

1. What is a big decision you have faced?

2. Did you think about the consequences of your decision?

3. What values influenced your decision?

4. Were you happy with your decision? What would you have done differently?

(TITLE)

A Play in One Act

Cast of Characters

A Synopsis

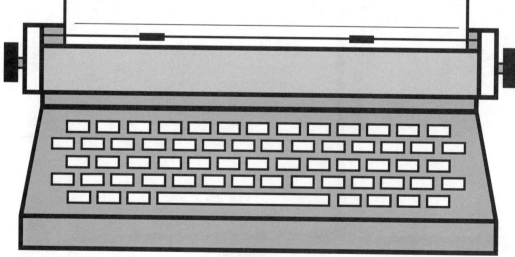

▶▶ **Faith Action**

Think back to the discussion you shared with a member of your class about decision making. If you are faced with a similar decision this week, try to put into practice what you have learned.

Morality: A Crossword Puzzle

When you choose to live your life in Christ, you use your gift of free will and intellect. Test your knowledge about making moral decisions and fill in the crossword.

 Clues

ACROSS

4. A sin we commit when we knowingly and freely choose something against but not in itself gravely against God's law

7. The how, who, when and where of a moral act

8. Our _____ and free will make us responsible for our actions.

10. The way of life for a group of people

11. The way we have been created to live

DOWN

1. The gift of God that helps us judge right from wrong

2. The part of a moral act that we choose to say or do

3. The original sense of right and wrong that is a part of every human being

5. The part of a moral act that considers why we choose to say or do something

6. A sin we commit when we turn our backs totally on God

9. To freely and knowingly do what is against God's law

 Faith Action

This week ask a friend or family member to describe their understanding of free will. Tell them what you have learned and compare your views with theirs.

Signs of a Christian Life

Design the blank road signs and let them become road signs for your life journey as a follower of Christ. Place on each sign key words or phrases that will remind you of the steps to a well-informed moral decision. Think about how each word or phrase might affect your decisions in the future.

 Faith Action

Cut out the box of completed road signs. Place it where you can refer to it on a daily basis to help you make decisions to live as a follower of Jesus.

Knowing Paul: A Word Game

The terms in the word bank are all associated with Saint Paul's First Letter to the Corinthians. Regroup the terms into four categories. Then write one or more sentences, using the terms in each category to reflect a true statement about Saint Paul's First Letter to the Corinthians.

Gentiles	factions	seaport	lower class	Jews
love	farmlands	heal	Greeks	Paul
evangelized	patience	Corinth	Apollos	greatest gift
Mediterranean	Cephas	trade	new commandment	Baptism

Faith Action

Read 1 Corinthians 13 from a Bible with your family this week. Discuss together how your family can show this kind of love for one another.

An Evangelist's Message: An Acrostic

Reflect on Saint Paul's teaching that living a life of love is at the heart of living as a disciple of Christ. Use each letter in the word *evangelize* to create a poem that reflects Paul's teaching on love. Each line of the poem should begin with the letter of the word. Your poem does not have to rhyme but should focus on the theme.

E _____

V _____

A _____

N _____

G _____

E _____

L _____

I _____

Z _____

E _____

 Faith Action

Think of someone who has helped you come to know the Gospel. Choose a way to follow their example and share the Good News with someone this week.

Virtues: Practice Makes Perfect

Christian living requires practice. Virtues are spiritual habits or behaviors that help you make wise decisions to do what is right and avoid what is wrong. For each of the virtues below, write its definition and then cut out the boxes to create flash cards. On the blank side of each card draw a symbol that reflects the meaning of the virtue. Take turns showing your symbols to a partner to test each other's knowledge of the theological and cardinal virtues.

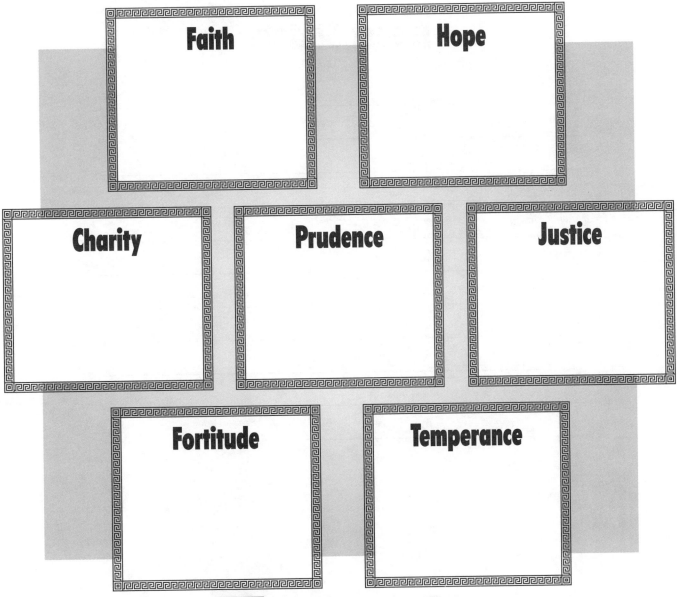

Faith

Hope

Charity

Prudence

Justice

Fortitude

Temperance

 Faith Action

Virtues must be practiced. Choose one of the virtues on this page. Make a commitment to respond to some situation this week in a way that shows you are living this virtue.

Creating a Just Society

The exercise of virtue helps create a just society. With two other classmates, brainstorm ways you can help create a just society. List your ideas on the globe. Keep your ideas practical and include ideas you can carry out this week.

A Just Society

 Faith Action

What is a roadblock that can keep you from acting justly in a certain situation? Take time this week to decide on a way to overcome that roadblock so that you will act justly.

God's Grace: A Concept Map

Deepening your understanding of God's gift of grace can help you to grow in faith, hope, and love. Develop a concept map that describes God's gift of grace. Share your map with a partner and compare your ideas. Discuss your ideas about ways grace can help you to grow in faith, hope, and love.

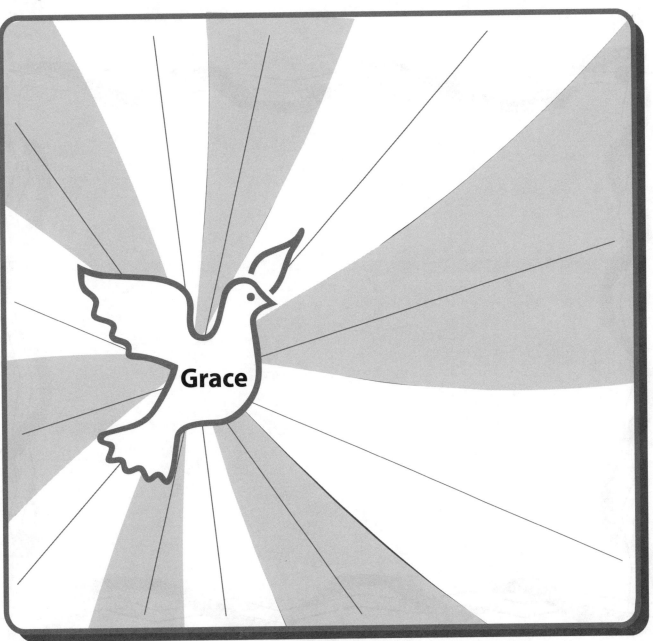

 Faith Action

Think of someone you know whom you or others have treated unfairly in the past. Do something positive this week to show that you respect the dignity of this person.

Freedom Framed

People about to be baptized promise to reject sin and to live in freedom as God's children. Reflect on your God-given gift of freedom and your continued desire for freedom in your daily life. In the frame of freedom create your artistic interpretation of the term *freedom*. In other words draw *freedom*.

 Faith Action

Place your drawing of freedom on your refrigerator at home. When someone asks you about it, explain what true freedom is.

God's Law: A Crossword Puzzle

When the Israelites wandered through the desert feeling lost and hopeless, God revealed the Ten Commandments through Moses to guide them. The Ten Commandments help you travel your journey of faith each day. Complete the crossword. See how much you already know about the Ten Commandments.

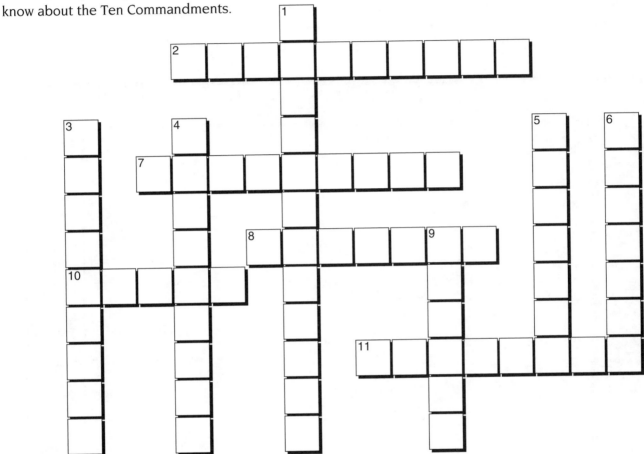

ACROSS

2. The foundation of all human laws engraved on the human heart

7. An attitude of profound respect

8. The rejection or denial of the existence of God

10. Things or people that take the place of God in our life

11. The worshiping of something or someone other than God

DOWN

1. The exaggerated belief that diverts us from trusting in God's loving providence

3. The mistreating of anyone or anything that is set aside for worshiping God

4. Means "ten words"; sets the foundation of our life with God

5. A rule or principle that imposes a standard of conduct or behavior on people

6. Calling on God to testify to a lie

9. The abuse of spiritual power for personal gain

▶▶ Faith Action

Think of one way that you and your family could do a better job of recreating your proper relationship with God and one another on Sundays. Share your idea with your family.

A Commandments Web Page

The Ten Commandments help us live our lives in Christ. The First, Second, and Third Commandments are about making and keeping God the priority in our lives. In the space below create a Web page that describes the first three Commandments, using contemporary examples and images that will appeal to young people. As you continue your study of the Ten Commandments in this unit, you may wish to add to the design of your Web page.

 Faith Action

Look at magazine ads aimed at young people with a friend or family member this week. Discuss the ads that make a material thing so important that it could become a kind of idol.

Discipleship: A Character Study

Martha and Mary were both loyal disciples of Jesus, yet they took different approaches to discipleship. Both approaches are necessary for discipleship. Place words or phrases associated with Martha in the top circle and those for Mary in the bottom circle. In the center where the circles overlap, put words or phrases that describe the ways Martha's and Mary's approach to discipleship are similar.

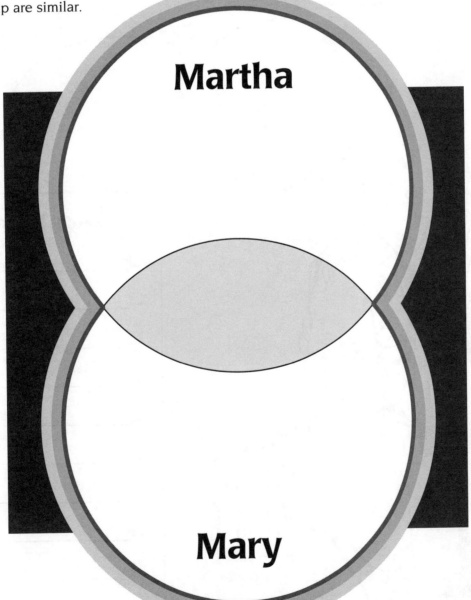

Martha

Mary

Faith Action

Decide two ways to be a disciple this week. Let your two decisions reflect ways of using the gifts of both Martha and Mary—service and prayerful listening.

Traveling Disciples

If you were going on a missionary journey to invite others to become disciples of Jesus, what would you take with you? What kind of gifts and talents would you need to pack? What kind of action words would you need to remember? Below is a drawing of traveling disciples. Draw their faces, list what they should carry in their luggage, and put words in their mouths. Label your drawing and be prepared to share it with your classmates.

Things to Take

- _____
- _____
- _____
- _____
- _____
- _____
- _____
- _____
- _____
- _____

Faith Action

Take the time this week to point out to at least one friend or family member a quality they have that marks them as a disciple of Jesus.

Respect: A Hidden Message

Figure out what words the clues represent. Then find the words in the grid. Words can go horizontally, vertically, and diagonally in all eight directions. When you are finished, the unused letters in the grid will spell out a hidden message. Start from the upper left, and pick out the unused letters from left to right in each row. You will not need any letters in the last four rows. Write the message on a card. Discuss with a partner how the message guides you in making decisions to live as a disciple of Jesus.

Clues

- ❖ Executing people for certain crimes
- ❖ Intentional killing of an unborn child
- ❖ Direct and intentional killing of a suffering person

- ❖ Penalty for performing or assisting at an abortion
- ❖ Thou shall not kill
- ❖ First word of the Fourth Commandment
- ❖ Direct and intentional killing of an innocent person

- ❖ Respectful listening and trusting response to a person with just authority over us
- ❖ Intentional and direct killing of oneself

```
C  F  I  F  T  H  C  O  M  M  A  N  D  M  E  N  T
H  R  I  S  T  E  I  A  N  S  A  R  E  C  N  A  N
E  L  L  E  D  T  C  O  H  O  N  O  R  O  A  N  E
X  D  O  B  E  Y  T  N  H  O  S  E  I  I  N  A  M
C  U  T  H  O  R  I  T  E  Y  W  T  H  O  A  R  H
O  E  R  E  S  E  P  O  N  I  R  S  I  B  L  E  S
M  F  E  O  R  O  U  U  R  O  D  G  R  O  W  T  I
M  H  D  A  N  D  W  T  B  E  L  E  L  B  E  I  N
U  N  I  G  A  N  D  A  H  A  R  E  B  E  X  P  U
N  E  C  C  T  E  T  D  T  A  O  H  O  O  N  O  P
I  R  I  A  L  C  L  H  U  M  N  A  N  L  I  F  L
C  E  U  A  E  H  S  A  S  A  C  A  R  E  D  G  A
A  I  S  R  O  F  T  F  R  O  M  G  S  O  D  N  T
T  M  I  N  T  M  K  J  K  J  J  X  R  I  W  D  I
I  D  O  K  T  R  E  D  R  U  M  N  B  W  A  B  P
O  R  P  G  N  X  T  D  L  H  M  N  T  L  K  R  A
N  N  G  L  D  X  P  H  L  Q  M  G  T  R  C  T  C
```

Faith Action

Practice the skill of peacemaking this week. At the end of each day, reflect back on the ways that you did so and thank God for the grace that allowed you to do his will.

A Fourth-Commandment Dilemma

The Fourth Commandment commands you to obey your parents and those in charge of your well-being. Look at this dilemma of a young eighth grader. Using the Fourth Commandment decide what she should do.

Grace's Dilemma

Grace has wanted to be friends with a popular group in her class for a long time. One day one of the girls, Jenna, invites Grace to a sleepover party. However, one of the other girls who is invited confides to Grace at lunch that Jenna's parents will be away overnight. She also tells her that Jenna has invited some boys to come over and watch TV with them in the evening. Grace still wants to go but hesitates because her mother and father have a firm rule that she cannot sleep over with her girlfriends if their parents are not home. The other girl tells Jenna to stop being a baby and grow up. She explains that they do this all the time, no one ever finds out, and they always have a good time. What should Grace do? Discuss this dilemma with a friend. Then respond to the questions.

STOP!
If you were in Grace's situation, what would your feelings be? What questions would be in your mind?

_____

_____

_____

LISTEN!
Who could help Grace make her decision? Whose advice can she trust?

_____

_____

_____

LOOK!
What are Grace's options? What could be the consequences of each decision? In each choice, who would be helped and who would be hurt?

_____

_____

_____

GO!
What do you think Grace should do? Why?

_____

_____

_____

▶▶ Faith Action

Now that you are growing older, you can take more responsibility for contributing to your family. This week suggest an attitude or action that would make your family stronger. Be sure to practice it yourself.

Guiding Your Conscience with the Commandments

Studying the Ten Commandments will help you build a healthy conscience. A healthy conscience can help guide your decisions. After reviewing the Sixth, Seventh, and Ninth Commandments, fill in the chart using the terms in the word bank. Then use the words in one of the columns to write one or more sentences about that Commandment.

respect	Life and love	balance	reparation
lifelong marriage	modesty	temperance	fornication
covet	faithful	liberate	stealing
hoard	justice	chastity	honor
Sexuality	responsibility	homosexual practices	profit
adultery	modesty	power	contraception
trial marriage	premarital sex	common good	stewardship
share	defend	oppress	domination

Sixth and Ninth Commandment		Seventh Commandment	
Living the Commandment	Against the Commandment	Living the Commandment	Against the Commandment

_____

_____

_____

_____

 Faith Action

Watch a TV show or music video with your family this week. Discuss the values that are portrayed on the show or video and how they compare with the values of Jesus.

Character Campaigns

Chastity. Reflect for a moment on the virtue of chastity. Think about the importance and need to live a chaste lifestyle. In the circle create a campaign button that encourages young people to live a chaste life. Use symbols, shapes, and color in your creation.

Stewardship. Radio stations air a certain number of public service announcements for the listening communities they serve. Outline your ideas for one related to "Respect for God's Creation." Include a catchy campaign jingle that will attract the notice of listeners.

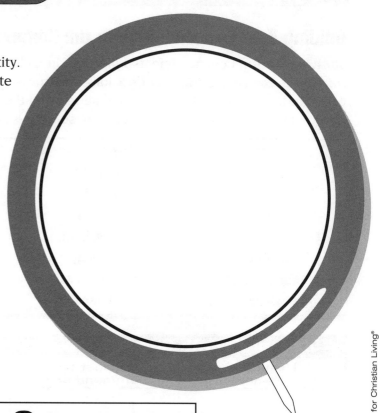

RESPECT FOR GOD'S CREATION

JINGLE: _____

_____

OUTLINE OF ANNOUNCEMENT: _____

_____

_____

_____

_____

_____

 Faith Action

The call to stewardship includes a concern for the quality of public life. This week take the time to read an article about a current local political issue. Write a letter to a public official expressing your Christian viewpoint on the issue.

Truth and Generosity: In Your Own Words

The Eighth and Tenth Commandments teach about truth and generosity. The words in the five boxes relate to actions that are opposed to these two Commandments. To help you remember what you have learned about the Eighth and Tenth Commandments, create one or two sentences that show the "flip side" of the negative words in the boxes. The first one is done for you as an example.

| deceive |
| disguise |
| deny |

Darla decided that owning up to what she had done was the only way to repair her reputation.

| gossip |
| calumny |
| detraction |

_____

_____

_____

| lying |
| perjury |
| boasting |

_____

_____

_____

| coveting |
| avarice |
| greed |

_____

_____

_____

| collusion |
| bullying |
| peer pressure |

_____

_____

_____

Faith Action

Each night this week, recall each of the Ten Commandments and ask yourself how well you have loved and served God and others as the Ten Commandments call you to do.

A Dialogue About Honesty

You have learned that the Eighth Commandment teaches about the responsibility to honor the reputation of others, to respect confidences, and to avoid exaggerating your own accomplishments. Use the questions to interview a classmate and be interviewed by a classmate about the Eighth Commandment. Write the responses in the space provided.

Interview Questions

1. What are some of the challenges you face to be honest?

2. When have you been tempted to exaggerate your own accomplishments? What did you do and why?

3. When have you been part of a conversation where someone was talked about behind their back? How did you feel?

4. Have you ever revealed a secret you were asked to keep? Is there ever a good reason to do so?

 Faith Action

Reflect back on your own response to the first interview question. Decide how you will respond to one of the challenges you have faced in acting with honesty and generosity.

A Morality Mobile

Below are seven circles with seven sets of words from the Our Father written on them. Cut out each circle and draw a picture or write a headline for a magazine or newspaper on the back that defines each phrase. When you have completed the seven circles, attach a thread to the circles and tie them on a hanger or dowel to create a mobile.

Hallowed Be Thy **Name**

Our **Father** in Heaven

Thy **Kingdom** Come

Give Us **This** Day Our **Daily Bread**

Thy **Will** be Done **on Earth** as It is in **Heaven**

Lead Us Not Into Temptation But **Deliver Us** From Evil

Forgive Us Our Trespasses As We Forgive Those Who **Trespass** Against Us

Faith Action

The Lord's Prayer makes the Gospel come alive for us. Pray the Lord's Prayer three times each day this week and reflect on the words as you do so.

A Mirror-Image Disciple

The Lord's Prayer provides a portrait of discipleship. In the top half of the mirror draw or write a description of yourself. In the lower half of the mirror draw or write a description of someone who lives the Lord's Prayer. On the dividing line write one thing that will help you become a better mirror image of a disciple of Jesus.

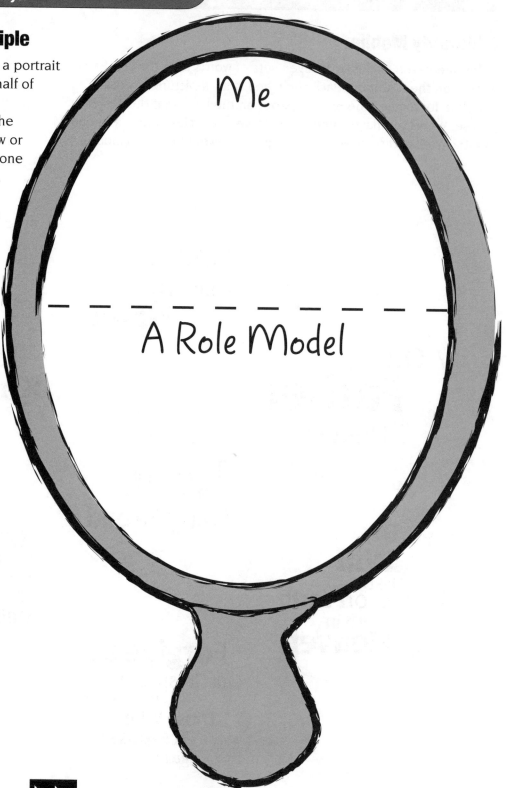

Me

A Role Model

Faith Action

Look back on the thing that you said would help you become a better mirror image of discipleship. Make a decision to practice doing that thing in the week ahead. Expressing your decision to a friend or family member may help you to follow through on putting your decision into action.

Morality

Answer Key for Activities

Chapter 1
Human Dignity and Happiness

Page 7: The Way to Happiness: A Word Search

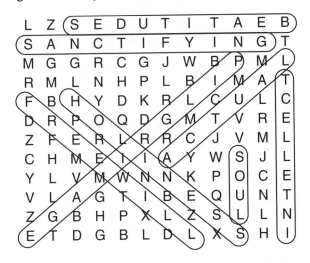

Page 8: My Blueprint for Happiness

Affirm all appropriate responses. Student responses should reflect an understanding of the Beatitudes and the true meaning of happiness revealed and taught by Jesus.

Chapter 2
One Person's Decision: A Scripture Story

Page 9: Four-Square Vocabulary: Disciple

1. **Define the term using the textbook definition.** A disciple is someone who follows a teacher. A disciple places total unconditional trust in God the Father as Jesus did.

2. **Define the term in your own words.** Affirm all appropriate responses.

3. **Use the term in a sentence.** Affirm all appropriate responses.

4. **Draw a picture to define the term.** Affirm all appropriate responses.

Page 10: Making Decisions: A Short Play

Affirm all appropriate responses.

Chapter 3
The Decision to Live Our Life in Christ

Page 11: Morality: A Crossword Puzzle

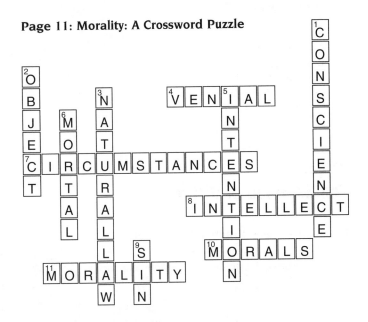

Page 12: Signs of a Christian Life

Affirm all appropriate responses.

Chapter 4
Hymn of Love: A Scripture Story

Page 13: Knowing Paul: A Word Game

Possible groups:

1	2	3	4
Gentiles	Corinth	factions	love
Greeks	Mediterranean	Apollos	greatest gift
lower class	farmlands	Cephas	heal
Jews	seaport	Paul	patience
Baptism	trade	evangelize	new commandment

Affirm all appropriate sentences that students construct. Possible sentences related to each group might be:

1. Saint Paul evangelized many Jews, Greeks, and other Gentiles in Corinth and many of them asked for Baptism.

2. Corinth was a seaport center of trade on the Mediterranean Sea, surrounded by mountains and farmlands.

3. After Saint Paul evangelized the Corinthians, many members of the early Church in Corinth split into factions around the person who had first proclaimed the Gospel to them—Paul, Apollos, or Cephas.

4. Saint Paul taught the Corinthians that it is Jesus' new commandment of love that can teach them patience and help them heal their divisions.

Answer Key for Activities

Page 14: An Evangelist's Message: An Acrostic

Affirm all appropriate poems. Sample:

Evangelize!
Voices together,
All as one,
Naming always
God's Son, Jesus.
Evangelize!
Let your voices rise
In love for the Lord—
Zenith of all our hopes.
Evangelize!

Chapter 5

The Exercise of Virtue

Page 15: Virtues: Practice Makes Perfect

The illustrations will vary, but must include a correct interpretation of the definition. Possible responses:

Faith
A theological virtue. God's invitation to believe in him and our ability to respond to his invitation.

Hope
A theological virtue. Helps us keep our eyes on the kingdom of God. Helps us trust in God.

Charity
A theological virtue. Helps us love God and our neighbor as ourselves because of our love for God.

Prudence
A cardinal virtue. Practical wisdom that helps us choose what is good.

Justice
A cardinal virtue. Helps us respect the rights of others

Temperance
A cardinal virtue. Helps us exercise moderation and self control.

Fortitude
A cardinal virtue. Gives us strength and the ability to stand up for what is right and good.

Page 16: Creating a Just Society

Affirm all appropriate responses.

Chapter 6

The Grace of the Holy Spirit

Page 17: God's Grace: A Concept Map

Concept maps are effective ways to organize graphically new material and ideas. They allow students who learn visually to deepen their understanding of a concept through critical thinking and visually representing the material.

Affirm all appropriate responses that could include such concepts as: seed, love, freely shared, abundant life, deepest desire of our hearts, strength to find happiness, live in freedom, sanctifying, actual, infused at baptism, love of God, healing, restoring holiness, Holy Spirit.

Page 18: Freedom Framed

Affirm all appropriate responses.

Chapter 7

The First, Second, and Third Commandments

Page 19: God's Law: A Crossword Puzzle

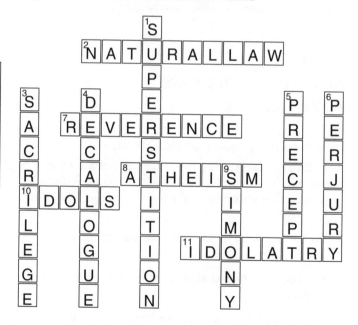

Page 20: A Commandments Web Page

Affirm all appropriate responses.

Answer Key for Activities

Chapter 8
Martha and Mary: A Scripture Story

Page 21: Discipleship: A Character Study
Affirm all appropriate responses.

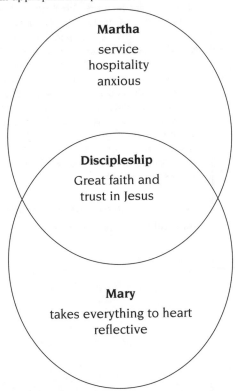

Martha
service
hospitality
anxious

Discipleship
Great faith and
trust in Jesus

Mary
takes everything to heart
reflective

Page 22: Traveling Disciples
Affirm all appropriate responses. Remind the young people that things to take might include attributes, virtues, and qualities, as well as material objects.

Chapter 9
The Fourth and Fifth Commandments

Page 23: Respect: A Hidden Message

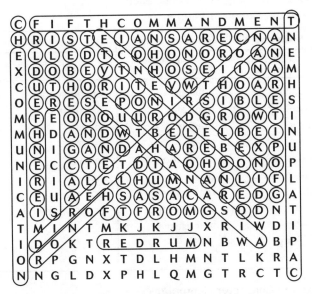

Hidden Message:
Christians are called to honor and obey those in authority who are responsible for our growth and well-being and are expected to honor all human life as a sacred gift from God.

Page 24: A Fourth Commandment Dilemma
Affirm all appropriate responses. Possible responses:

Stop! Feelings: fear, anxiety, excitement; Questions: What if I get caught? What will my parents think? Does Jenna ever get scared? Why does Jenna have to break the rules? Why are my parents so strict?

Look! *Option* 1: Grace goes along and hopes not to be caught. *Consequences* 1: Worry, disappointment and shame, and guilt.
Helped: Only temporary gains—in the end, no one is helped.
Hurt: Grace, by violating her own values; parents, by showing them disrespect.
Option 2: Grace refuses to break family rules and stays home. *Consequences* 2: Grace's family is strengthened; Jenna learns a lesson; Grace grows stronger and holier through her decision.

Listen! Who could help? Parents or other trusted caregivers; teacher or catechist; priest; older sibling; God, through his grace.

Go! Refuse to go and all the positive consequences of Option 2 are realized.

Answer Key for Activities

Chapter 10
The Sixth, Seventh and Ninth Commandments

Page 25: Guiding Your Conscience with the Commandments

Sixth and Ninth Commandment		Seventh Commandment	
Living the Commandment	Against the Commandment	Living the Commandment	Against the Commandment
sexuality	adultery	common good	power
life and love	fornication	stewardship	domination
balance	premarital sex	liberate	oppress
lifelong marriage	covet	justice	abuse
modesty	domination	defend	hoard
temperance	power	share	profit
faithful	trial marriage	reparation	stealing
honor	contraception	responsibility	cheating
chastity	homosexual practices		
modesty			

Page 26: Character Campaigns
Affirm all appropriate responses.

Chapter 11
The Eighth and Tenth Commandments

Page 27: Truth and Generosity: In Your Own Words

Affirm all appropriate responses. Sample sentences:

We can break the Eighth Commandment when we deceive others, disguise our true feelings in order to deceive someone, or deny something that we know to be true.

Gossip can lead to calumny by making others doubt someone's good reputation or to detraction by revealing faults that would not otherwise be known.

Boasting is related to lying because it exaggerates the truth about oneself, and lying becomes perjury if it happens under oath.

Coveting other people's possessions can lead to avarice and greed.

Peer pressure can lead to bullying and collusion—a conspiracy against others for a negative purpose.

Page 28: A Dialogue About Honesty

Affirm all appropriate responses. Remind the students that the sharing between partners should be held in confidence unless the information shared can bring harm. Remind them that the keeping of confidences is a way that we keep the Eighth Commandment.

Chapter 12
The Lord's Prayer

Page 29: A Morality Mobile

Affirm all appropriate responses. Possible images might include: **Our Father:** image of a loving father; **Hallowed:** person praying; decorated letters of the name YHWH, **Thy Kingdom come:** image depicting peace, harmony, or justice; **Thy will be done:** image of a person doing good works; **Give us our daily Bread:** food image or image of a person performing a virtuous act; **Forgive us:** image of reconciliation among people or of the sacrament of Reconciliation; **Lead us not:** image of Holy Spirit or Resurrection of Jesus, or image of a person engaged in a wholesome activity.

Page 30: A Mirror-Image Disciple

Affirm all appropriate responses.

Assessment Tools

About This Section

This section begins with some introductory pages on the theory of assessment, followed by the chapter and unit tests. As you read, you'll find that the *Faith First Legacy Edition* philosophy encourages you to assess the many ways that the young people in your care are growing in the knowledge of their faith and in their ability to apply this knowledge to daily life. Here is an overview of the features in the pages that follow.

Introduction

An overview of the *Faith First Legacy Edition* holistic approach to assessment

Assessment Tools in the Student Book

A summary of the various features in *Faith First Legacy Edition* that contribute to an overall student assessment

Faith First Testing Strategies

An explanation of the kinds of test questions used in the *Faith First Legacy Edition* chapter and unit assessments

Developing Rubrics

A summary of the value of establishing rubrics that affirm the students' involvement in the learning process

Levels of Thinking

An explanation of the six levels of thinking in Benjamin Bloom's taxonomy and suggested questioning strategies to support them

Using Portfolios

An explanation of the role of portfolios in assessing student progress

Chapter and Unit Assessments

Twenty-six two-page chapter assessments and two four-page unit assessments that can be used for in-class evaluation or for a more comprehensive review at home with the student's family

Answer Key

A comprehensive key to guide your evaluation of the chapter and unit assessments

Reminder: All pages in this activity and assessment booklet are reproducible for classroom use.

Introduction to Assessment

Think for a moment about how you were assessed as a student. Many of us thought that multiple-choice, true or false, and fill-in-the-blank questions were the only ways our teachers evaluated what we had learned. Today we realize that to assess our students' strengths as learners, it is better to see assessment as an ongoing process and an integral part of all our teaching and catechizing.

Since students have different styles for learning and ways they best express their learning, assessment must incorporate multiple strategies. *Faith First Legacy Edition* uses a variety of both formal and informal tools to help young people demonstrate what they have learned and how they are applying it in daily life. This ability allows them to understand more clearly who they are as growing persons of faith.

The *Faith First Legacy Edition* and its assessment component encourage teachers/catechists to be creative and to use multiple strategies to enhance and evaluate student learning. Through the use of a wide range of classroom activities, discussions, reviews, test questions, and portfolios, *Faith First Legacy* provides a holistic approach to assessment. Using these strategies, young people will develop a deeper understanding of the story of faith and learn to value their faith as an integral part of daily living.

Assessment provides a way of comparing student achievement against established goals and objectives. By doing so, we may need to change our modes of instruction. Also, multiple forms of assessment allow us to provide for individual differences.

Religious education assessment is a form of communication among students, teachers/catechists, and the wider faith community. It is

Assessment

- ☐ a measure of the knowledge acquired
- ☐ part of all teaching and learning
- ☐ ongoing
- ☐ a movement through different levels of thinking
- ☐ a means of leading learners to use knowledge in daily life
- ☐ an interactive process between teacher/catechist and learner
- ☐ an opportunity for growth in faith

a way to communicate that the traditions of our faith are indeed being passed on from one generation to another.

No matter what we do in life we are accountable for our words and actions. In the same way, as teachers and catechists we are accountable for our students' growth in knowledge of their faith. The more our students learn about their faith, the more they can understand the difference faith makes in their lives. We have learned in our own lives that a deeper knowledge of the story of faith has enhanced our relationship with God and our appreciation of our Catholic tradition. It only makes sense, then, that as students gain a deeper understanding of their faith story, they'll have a better opportunity to cultivate a deeper relationship with God and a sense of what it means to be a committed Catholic.

Assessment Tools in the Student Book

The student books are probably the best illustration of the *Faith First Legacy* assessment philosophy. From cover to cover, the *Faith First Legacy Edition* student books have built-in features to help you assess student progress in both informal and formal ways.

Your teacher/catechist guide offers you strategies for using your student book successfully by incorporating the various ways young people learn. This allows you to honor your students' individuality and give them the opportunity to express their learning in the way that is best for them. Each of these strategies gives you an additional lens through which you can evaluate the young people's understanding and application of the lesson content.

"Welcome to Faith First!"

The opening lesson includes an activity to help you and the students get acquainted with one another's life experiences. A two-page activity follows that forecasts the grade level content and allows you to see what the students already know about some key points.

Unit Openers

The four unit openers help you assess what the young people's prior knowledge is of the unit subject matter. The pictures on the opening page offer visual prompts to activate their memory of what they have learned earlier. The second page continues to question them about their prior knowledge. They are also asked to write one question that they hope the unit will answer.

Engage

An opening exercise in each chapter of the text includes a life experience question and a question to activate prior knowledge that are both related to the chapter topic.

Teach and Apply

The "Faith Focus" question helps learners begin to think about the main chapter concept. In-text factual, interpretive, and applied questioning strategies help teachers/catechists assess comprehension and the ability to apply knowledge to daily life. On-page activities help young people apply what they are learning to life situations.

"What Difference Does Faith Make?"

An activity invites students to think of ways to apply the chapter concept to a life situation. The students use their knowledge to make decisions. Students then make a "Faith Choice"—a concrete choice to respond in a personal way to the chapter content.

"We Remember"

The "To Help You Remember" feature helps the students recall three main points of each chapter. The review activity assesses the religious vocabulary that the students have gained and helps you monitor how well they have acquired the faith concepts of the chapter.

Unit Reviews

The unit reviews help you and the young people assess what they have learned about faith vocabulary words, chapter concepts, and an important Scripture story. By mirroring the approach of the unit openers, the unit reviews help the students see how they are adding to their faith knowledge as the year progresses.

Faith First Testing Strategies

Four principles guided the development of the questions used in the *Faith First* assessment tools in this booklet. The tests:

- reflect the most important concepts in the chapter.

- assess in a manner similar to the teaching/learning process in the student books.

- provide a variety of test items in choices to evaluate understanding from different viewpoints.

- lead the students to incorporate the knowledge into their lives.

Chapter Tests

The *Faith First* chapter and unit tests include five categories of test questions that are developmentally appropriate for the grade level of the students. Each level helps the learner grow through the different levels of thinking.

- "Faith Vocabulary" evaluates the learners' understanding and usage of their growing faith vocabulary.

- "Remembering Our Faith" helps the learners identify basic information about their faith beliefs. This section includes multiple choice or true or false statements.

- "Understanding Our Faith" provides a tool for the learners to express an understanding of the concepts in their own words. The answer key will guide your grading of this section by offering main points that their responses might or should include.

- "Living Our Faith" helps the learners internalize their new knowledge in a way that allows for explanation, empathy, interpretation,

Key Feature

A key feature of the "Remembering Our Faith" section in grades 5–8 is the inclusion of a multiple choice testing strategy that is commonly used in the **A.C.R.E. Assessment Program** from NCEA and in some standardized diocesan testing tools. Children who become familiar with this style of testing year by year have a better opportunity for success on standardized tests.

application, perspective, and self-knowledge. This question helps students extend their thinking about the chapter concepts and tell how it will make a difference in their lives. All student responses to this question should be considered correct as long as they reflect comprehension of the question concept. You might even invite them to respond through drawing or some other creative art form.

Unit Tests

The unit tests follow the format of the chapter tests and incorporate two additional questions. The "What I'll Remember" feature asks the students to recall a chapter concept or person of faith in the unit that made a particular impression on them and to tell why. The "Portfolio" feature is for students who have been asked to create portfolios of their work week by week. This feature invites them to look back through their portfolio and to comment on what they consider to be their best or most meaningful work in the past unit. These last two features are really a student self-assessment tool and should not be included in the test grade.

Developing Rubrics

A rubric is simply a set of specific criteria for scoring student work. It contains descriptions of varying levels of achievement and understanding. Elementary and junior high children need feedback and appreciate knowing how well they are doing in each of their classes. As the students work through each chapter, it is important to provide them with criteria that affirm their involvement in the faith learning process.

Remember that there is a limit to what tests and the rubrics to measure progress can do. One's relationship with God ultimately is deeply personal and only God can see what goes on in an individual's heart. Rubrics are simply criteria to measure external indicators. The next page is an example of a rubric that you might share with your learners and use as a basis for grading. It is but one tool that might be used to assess a student's engagement in learning. Review the rubric occasionally with the students. As each chapter is completed, use the rubric to assess what standard each student has achieved in this chapter. This rubric uses a 4 to 1 scale. If your program uses letter grades, you can easily adapt this rubric to that system. Extra lines have been added for you to add any expectations specific to your program.

The Value of Rubrics

- ☐ Focus on specific criteria

- ☐ Provide objectivity in assessing the students' knowledge of their faith tradition

- ☐ Provide students with ownership of their learning

- ☐ Provide students, teachers, and parents with a measurable tool to evaluate student progress in the acquisition of faith knowledge and the external expression of faith experience

- ☐ Allow for self, peer, and teacher evaluation

- ☐ Allow for students to evaluate their strengths and areas for growth

- ☐ Provide quality expectations that can yield quality work

- ☐ Enhance the self-confidence and religious identity of students

- ☐ Improve skill levels

Involvement in Learning About My Faith

Student's Name _____ Chapter_____

4 ____ Participates in prayer; consistently asks and answers questions; leads and contributes to partner, group, and class discussions; utilizes the activities to suggest differences faith makes in his or her daily life; excels at chapter reviews

_____
_____
_____

3 ____ Participates in prayer; asks and answers some questions; contributes to partner, group, and class discussions; completes the activities; completes the chapter reviews

_____
_____
_____

2 ____ Participates in prayer; answers questions when asked; passively contributes to the partner, group, and class discussions; completes most activities; needs assistance with chapter reviews

_____
_____
_____

1 ____ Participates in prayer; seldom interacts with questions and answers; does not participate in the partner, group, and class discussions; seldom completes activities; does not complete chapter reviews

_____
_____
_____

Total: ____ Comments: _____

_____
_____
_____

Throughout the *Faith First* program there are opportunities for students to complete enrichment projects and activities. The "Enriching the Lesson" feature at the end of every chapter in the teacher/catechist guide offers three choices for every chapter that can be completed in or out of class, alone or with friends and family. Some of the activities and projects reinforce learning while others extend it. Here is an example of a rubric you might use. Be sure to discuss this rubric with the young people before the project begins.

Involvement in Religion Projects

Student's Name _____ Chapter_____

4 _____ Extends the learning of the concepts of the chapter; uses a variety of resources to acquire information (print material, Internet, surveys); presents information in various forms, such as art projects, song, drama, computers, overheads, charts; completes a project that reflects pride and professional appearance

3 _____ Extends the learning of the concepts of the chapter; uses an outside resource such as the Internet to acquire information; presents information in appropriate form; completes an accomplished project

2 _____ Reinforces the learning of the concepts of the chapter; uses information already presented in the chapter; presents information; completes project

1 _____ Reinforces the learning of the concepts of the chapter; uses insufficient information; presents information in a disorganized manner; does not complete project

Total: _____ Comments: _____

_____

_____

Levels of Thinking

One of the goals of religious education is to help children move to higher levels of thinking about their faith. Some of the most important research in this area, led by an educator named Benjamin Bloom, was completed in 1956. The research has come to be known as Bloom's taxonomy, which is simply an orderly classification of ideas. There are particular kinds of questions that support each of the six levels of thinking.

Faith First Legacy Edition makes use of this research to help children advance in their thinking about their faith. The chart below offers you a list of the levels of thinking in Bloom's taxonomy, some questioning strategies for each, and an example of this questioning that can be found in the components of the *Faith First Legacy Edition*.

Levels of Thinking in *Faith First Legacy*

Level of Thinking	Questioning Strategies	*Faith First* Examples
Knowledge *Cognitive recall of information*	List; define; describe; who, when, what, where; match; tell; identify; name	Name the day each year when the Church honors all the saints of heaven.
Comprehension *Understanding the meaning of information*	Compare or contrast, predict, summarize, discuss, group, explain, restate	Explain why living the Ten Commandments is important.
Application *Apply learning to new situations to solve problems*	Show or demonstrate, relate, change, discover, solve, chart, prepare	Look at the picture and tell a better way for the children to solve the problem.
Analysis *Breaking information down into component parts to make inferences or see patterns*	Classify, arrange, correlate, outline, diagram, prioritize, divide, illustrate, connect, explain why	Make a word map describing what you know about the word *disciple*.
Synthesis *Apply prior knowledge to produce a new idea*	Combine, rearrange, substitute, create or design, rewrite, compose, compile, plan, adapt	Design a new tabernacle for your church that shows how much we honor the Holy Eucharist.
Evaluation *Judge subjectively the value of new knowledge*	Conclude, critique, defend, interpret, justify, support, choose, verify	Why is it important to pray?

Using Portfolios

A portfolio is a collection of student work that demonstrates an understanding of the concepts being taught. Together, teachers or catechists and learners analyze and select the products week by week that will show growth in understanding. There are various activities throughout the *Faith First Legacy Edition* that may be used for portfolio assessment.

Journals. One important tool in portfolio assessment is a journal. A faith journal can show the student's response to both the cognitive and affective goals of learning. Students select one of the entries in the journal to show their growth in understanding and assimilating the faith concepts. Remember that journals are very personal documents. Invite the young people to choose possible entries to copy and add to the portfolio. Never read student journals without permission, unless you have alerted them at the outset that you will be reading them. Here are some open-ended statements you can use:

- When I imagine God, I see . . .
- If I could talk to Jesus right now, I would tell him that . . .
- The teaching of Jesus that is most important to me is . . .
- It is hard/easy for me to forgive when . . .

Activities. Another strategy is for students and teachers to select paper and pencil or art activities that best reflect the learners' understanding of the concepts. Many of the activities in the *Faith First Legacy Edition* lend themselves to this type of assessment. Students may remove or copy the activity from the book.

Portfolio Assessment

- ☐ Provides ongoing tangible evidence of understanding
- ☐ Guarantees consistent dialogue between teachers and learners
- ☐ Helps the learners assimilate their knowledge
- ☐ Involves the parents in young people's progress
- ☐ Enhances students' self-esteem

Audiotapes. Students tape their reflections about the chapter concepts. They also may invite peers, family, or community members to add similar reflections.

Other Modes of Creative Expression. The research in multiple intelligences encourages teachers to suggest a list of different ways students can demonstrate comprehension of the material. Using a variety of modes of expression is good for young people and helps to give teachers/catechists the fullest picture of young people's growth in faith understanding. Poetry, songs, art, plays, interviews, observations, and surveys may also be included in the portfolio. Teachers/catechists and students can work together to choose additions. Such activities also give the classroom teacher an indication of the young people's social skills, ability to engage in cooperative learning, and their insights into life and faith.

Tests or Chapter Reviews. Students can include tests and chapter reviews when they do very well on them or show marked improvement.

Morality

Faith Vocabulary

MATCH FAITH TERMS WITH THEIR MEANINGS. In each space provided, write the term that best fits the definition. There are more terms in the word box than you will need.

| sanctifying grace | holiness | soul | intellect | free will | actual grace | beatitude |

1. _____ the power to know God and to reflect on how God is a part of our lives

2. _____ the strengthening by the Holy Spirit that allows us to seek happiness by living a holy life

3. _____ the grace that makes us holy, or one with God

4. _____ the ability to love and serve God and choose to make God the center of our lives

5. _____ living our life in Christ

Remembering Our Faith

COMPLETE EACH SENTENCE. Insert the letter of the word or phrase that best completes each sentence.

6. The soul is _____.
   a. part of every human being
   b. spiritual and immortal
   c. the part of us that will never die
   d. all of the above

7. The Beatitudes that Jesus taught _____.
   a. take the place of the Ten Commandments
   b. identify the people and actions blessed by God
   c. describe happiness or blessedness
   d. both b and c

8. Jesus taught us that _____.
   a. holiness and happiness are not opposites
   b. it is better to be holy than to be happy
   c. holy people will not be happy until they go to heaven
   d. all of the above

9. A _____ is a spiritual journey.
   a. prayer
   b. pilgrimage
   c. beatitude
   d. chapel

10. Cardinal Bernardin's image of a "seamless garment" teaches us that _____.
    a. every single human life is important
    b. our work on behalf of the unborn, the disabled, the elderly, and the dying cannot be separated from one another
    c. human life must be respected at every stage of its existence
    d. all of the above

TRUE OR FALSE. Write T next to the statements that are true. Write F next to the statements that are false.

11. _____ Awe and wonder, which are Gifts of the Holy Spirit, give us the vision to see the beauty and holiness of human life.

12. _____ From the moment of our conception, we are destined to enjoy life with God forever.

13. _____ We will only be happy when we choose to make God the center of our lives.

14. _____ Happiness and holiness are opposites.

15. _____ God has left us on our own to figure out how to live our life in Christ.

Understanding Our Faith

TELL WHAT YOU HAVE LEARNED IN THIS CHAPTER. Write a two-sentence reflection for each of these items.

16. What is the source of the dignity and sacredness of every human person?

   _____

   _____

17. Compare holiness and happiness.

   _____

   _____

18. What is the role of the Holy Spirit in our search for happiness?

   _____

   _____

19. How do the Beatitudes guide us in living holy lives?

   _____

   _____

Living Our Faith

WRITE A SHORT PARAGRAPH. Use a separate piece of paper for your answer.

20. What is a concrete choice teenage Catholics can make that would show they are choosing both happiness and holiness? Give reasons for your answer.

Faith Vocabulary

MATCH FAITH TERMS WITH THEIR MEANINGS. In each space provided, write the term that best fits the definition. There are more terms in the word box than you will need.

Evangelists	Gospels	homily	Ezekiel	the Twelve	eternal life
	Jeremiah	the prophets	writing style		

1. _____ the reward of being a disciple of Christ

2. _____ the first disciples chosen by Jesus

3. _____ source of the winged lion image used to describe Mark the Evangelist

4. _____ important technique to consider in understanding a Bible passage

5. _____ the inspired writers of the Gospels

Remembering Our Faith

COMPLETE EACH SENTENCE. Insert the letter of the word or phrase that best completes each sentence.

6. The Gospel according to Mark was first written for _____.

    a. the Apostles
    b. Jews who had become followers of Jesus
    c. Gentiles who had become followers of Jesus
    d. both b and c

7. The Gospel according to Mark was probably written in _____

    a. A.D. 50–56
    b. A.D. 57–63
    c. A.D. 64–70
    d. A.D. 71–77

8. In the Gospel story presented in this chapter, the wealthy young man asked Jesus, "Good Teacher, what must I do to _____?"

    a. pray
    b. really be happy
    c. inherit eternal life
    d. keep my wealth and follow you

9. By making the choice to follow Jesus the wealthy young man would _____.

    a. achieve happiness
    b. receive eternal life
    c. have to give up his possessions
    d. all the above

TRUE OR FALSE. Write T next to the statements that are true. Write F next to the statements that are false.

10. _____ The four Gospels were written immediately after the Resurrection.

11. _____ The writers of the four Gospels were inspired by the Holy Spirit.

12. _____ The followers of Christ for whom Mark wrote his account of the Gospel were living so comfortably that they had to be reminded about what being a disciple really meant.

13. _____ The wealthy young man was convinced by Jesus to follow him.

14. _____ Jesus asked his disciples to place total trust in God the Father as he himself did.

15. _____ The disciples of Jesus use a different measure of success on earth than most others do.

Understanding Our Faith

TELL WHAT YOU HAVE LEARNED IN THIS CHAPTER. Write a two-sentence reflection for each of these items.

16. In what way could Mark's Gospel story of the wealthy young man have brought comfort to his readers who were being persecuted?

_____

_____

17. What does Jesus ask of anyone who wishes to become his disciple?

_____

_____

18. What does Mark's writing style tell you about Jesus' mission?

_____

_____

19. Describe the successful life of a Christian.

_____

_____

Living Our Faith

WRITE A SHORT PARAGRAPH. Use a separate piece of paper for your answer.

20. Why do you think pursuing wealth might be an obstacle to living as a faithful follower of Jesus Christ?

Faith Vocabulary

MATCH FAITH TERMS WITH THEIR MEANINGS. In each space provided, write the term that best fits the definition. There are more terms in the word box than you will need.

| morals | morality | natural law | sin | freedom | conscience | venial sin |

1. _____ original sense of right and wrong that is part of every human being

2. _____ any action whereby we freely and knowingly do what is against God's law

3. _____ a word meaning "the way of life for a group of people"

4. _____ gift from God that is part of every human being that helps us judge right from wrong

5. _____ term that describes the way we have been created to live

Remembering Our Faith

COMPLETE EACH SENTENCE. Insert the letter of the word or phrase that best completes each sentence.

6. The object of a moral act is _____.
   a. the how, who, when, or where of an act
   b. why we choose to say or do something
   c. what we choose to say or do
   d. all of the above

7. With mortal sin _____.
   a. we turn our backs totally on God
   b. we do not always commit a grave offense
   c. we lose sanctifying grace
   d. both a and c

8. The intention of a moral act is _____.
   a. why we choose to say or do something
   b. what we choose to say or do
   c. not as important as the circumstances
   d. none of the above

9. Venial sin is _____.
   a. knowingly and freely choosing something against but not gravely against God's law
   b. not important
   c. so serious that we lose the gift of sanctifying grace
   d. both a and c

10. The circumstances of a moral act _____.
    a. make no difference
    b. determine if it is right or wrong in itself
    c. can increase its goodness or evil
    d. all of the above

TRUE OR FALSE. Write T next to the statements that are true. Write F next to the statements that are false.

11. _____ The Christian moral life is about freely choosing to respond to God the Father, Son, and Holy Spirit.

12. _____ Free will and intellect make us responsible for our own actions.

13. _____ Certain factors can impact both our freedom to choose and our responsibility for our choices.

14. _____ All sins turn our hearts away from God's love.

15. _____ Every human person is born with a well-formed conscience.

Understanding Our Faith

TELL WHAT YOU HAVE LEARNED IN THIS CHAPTER. Write a two-sentence reflection for each of these items.

16. What is natural law?

_____

_____

17. How can the Christian moral life be a path to freedom?

_____

_____

18. Describe the elements of a moral act. Give an example.

_____

_____

19. Why is it important to build a well-formed conscience?

_____

_____

Living Our Faith

WRITE A SHORT PARAGRAPH. Use a separate piece of paper for your answer.

20. What are some of the things you might say or do to show you take responsibility for your actions and their consequences?

Faith Vocabulary

MATCH FAITH TERMS WITH THEIR MEANINGS. In each space provided, write the term that best fits the definition. There are more terms in the word box than you will need.

evangelize	Corinth	love	Latin	Ephesus
faith	worship	Greek	persecution	write

1. _____ language in which Saint Paul's letters were originally written

2. _____ a seaport city in ancient Greece where Saint Paul founded a Christian community

3. _____ greatest of the virtues

4. _____ an important issue in the First Letter to the Corinthians

5. _____ to proclaim the Gospel to others, as Saint Paul did

Remembering Our Faith

COMPLETE EACH SENTENCE. Insert the letter of the word or phrase that best completes each sentence.

6. Paul evangelized the Corinthians during his _____ missionary journey.

   a. first
   b. second
   c. third
   d. fourth

7. The people living in Corinth who were baptized were _____ .

   a. Jews
   b. Gentiles
   c. a mixture of Jews and Gentiles
   d. none of the above

8. While in Corinth, Paul supported himself by working as a _____ .

   a. fisherman
   b. preacher
   c. tentmaker
   d. none of the above

9. _____ is at the heart of the message Saint Paul preached to the Corinthians.

   a. Courage
   b. Wisdom
   c. Love
   d. None of the above

10. The Letter to the _____ was probably written by a disciple of Saint Paul.

   a. Romans
   b. Ephesians
   c. First Corinthians
   d. none of the above

TRUE OR FALSE. Write T next to the statements that are true. Write F next to the statements that are false.

11. _____ Saint Paul advised the Corinthians to group around him or Apollos or Cephas as the source of their identity as followers of Christ.

12. _____ The use of the gifts of the Holy Spirit was the source of unity holding the followers of Christ in Corinth together.

13. _____ The gifts of the Holy Spirit are given for the good of the Body of Christ.

14. _____ In the First Letter to the Corinthians Saint Paul concludes that living a life of hope is at the heart of living as a disciple of Christ.

15. _____ Saint Paul declared that love is superior to all the other gifts of the Holy Spirit.

Understanding Our Faith

TELL WHAT YOU HAVE LEARNED IN THIS CHAPTER. Write a two-sentence reflection for each of these items.

16. Why did Saint Paul write the First Letter to the Corinthians?

_____

_____

17. What is the main point of 1 Corinthians 13:1–13?

_____

_____

18. What does Saint Paul remind us about the relationship of love to the other gifts of the Holy Spirit?

_____

_____

19. How does Saint Paul's advice to the Corinthians relate to Jesus' "new commandment"?

_____

_____

Living Our Faith

WRITE A SHORT PARAGRAPH. Use a separate piece of paper for your answer.

20. How does 1 Corinthians 13:1–13 help you live as a Christian?

Copyright © RCL • Resources for Christian Living®

Faith Vocabulary

MATCH FAITH TERMS WITH THEIR MEANINGS. In each space provided, write the term that best fits the definition. There are more terms in the word box than you will need.

virtues   common good   true authority   social sin   society
moral virtues   theological virtues

1. _____ a group of people distinct from other groups and sharing a common culture, common interests, and common activities

2. _____ individuals cooperating with one another to work against human life and human rights

3. _____ spiritual powers or habits or behaviors that help us do what is right and avoid what is wrong

4. _____ virtues that are also called cardinal virtues

5. _____ the strengths or habits that God gives us to help attain holiness

Remembering Our Faith

COMPLETE EACH SENTENCE. Insert the letter of the word or phrase that best completes each sentence.

6. The cardinal virtues include _____.
   a. prudence and justice
   b. temperance and love
   c. faith and hope
   d. love

7. _____ is the gift of God's invitation to believe in him.
   a. Prudence
   b. Hope
   c. Faith
   d. Courage

8. Charity is _____.
   a. love of God and neighbor
   b. the greatest of all the virtues
   c. the virtue that gives life and form to the other virtues
   d. all of the above

9. Virtues _____.
   a. help us make deliberate, knowledgeable decisions
   b. guide us in using our emotions and feelings to live as children of God
   c. give expression to our highest values
   d. all of the above

10. We are created to live together in a way that allows us to _____.
    a. resemble the Holy Trinity
    b. follow the Great Commandment
    c. work for the common good
    d. all of the above

**TRUE OR FALSE. Write T next to the statements that are true. Write F
next to the statements that are false.**

11. _____ The theological virtues are the pillars of our life in Christ because they
link us more closely to the Father, Son, and Holy Spirit.

12. _____ Our moral life and our moral decision making hinge on the development
and practice of the cardinal virtues.

13. _____ Human beings have been created by God as social creatures who are to live
as they wish.

14. _____ All authority flows from God.

15. _____ The Corporal Works of Mercy are laws society creates to support its own desires.

Understanding Our Faith

**TELL WHAT YOU HAVE LEARNED IN THIS CHAPTER. Write a two-sentence reflection for
each of these items.**

16. Describe the role of the theological virtues in the life of a Christian.

_____

_____

17. Describe each of the theological virtues.

_____

_____

18. Explain the function of civic, or social, authority.

_____

_____

19. Describe a just society.

_____

_____

Living Our Faith

WRITE A SHORT PARAGRAPH. Use a separate piece of paper for your answer.

20. Name and discuss a social sin and what you can do to work against it
to build a fair and just society.

Faith Vocabulary

MATCH FAITH TERMS WITH THEIR MEANINGS. In each space provided, write the term that best fits the definition. There are more terms in the word box than you will need.

| grace | justification | merit | sanctifying grace | sanctification | mercy |

1. _____ the process of restoring a person in right order or relationship with God

2. _____ the gift of God's life and love enabling us to live in communion with the Holy Trinity

3. _____ the divine work attributed to the Holy Spirit

4. _____ a free gift from God by which we are united with him and which empowers us to live as his children

5. _____ something we are worthy of or entitled to

Remembering Our Faith

COMPLETE EACH SENTENCE. Insert the letter of the word or phrase that best completes each sentence.

6. _____ restores our holiness.

   a. Merit
   b. Actual grace
   c. Sanctifying grace
   d. None of the above

7. _____ is the term the Church uses to describe Christ's work of setting us in right relationship with God.

   a. Justification
   b. Merit
   c. Both a and b
   d. None of the above.

8. The work of salvation has won for us the gift of _____.

   a. grace
   b. eternal life
   c. sanctifying grace
   d. all of the above

9. We merit God's grace because _____.

   a. we earn it
   b. we deserve it
   c. we need it
   d. none of the above

TRUE OR FALSE. Write T next to the statements that are true. Write F next to the statements that are false.

10. _____ Through faith in Jesus and Baptism we are justified.

11. _____ Before Christ's life, death, and Resurrection, humanity was under the power of sin and death.

12. _____ In Christ and through his Paschal Mystery all of creation is once again set in right relationship with God.

13. _____ New life in Christ is a gift we could never earn on our own.

14. _____ Jesus sent the Holy Spirit to us at his baptism.

15. _____ God freely gives us every blessing and grace we have because we deserve them.

Understanding Our Faith

TELL WHAT YOU HAVE LEARNED IN THIS CHAPTER. Write a two-sentence reflection for each of these items.

16. Describe the divine work of sanctification.

_____

_____

17. Describe the gift of justification.

_____

_____

18. Explain why we cannot earn the gift of our salvation solely by our own efforts.

_____

_____

19. Compare our seeking the kingdom of God with our living a life of holiness.

_____

_____

Living Our Faith

Write a short paragraph for your answer.

20. What are some of the ways you can put grace into action?

Morality

Faith Vocabulary

MATCH FAITH TERMS WITH THEIR MEANINGS. In each space provided, write the term that best fits the definition. There are more terms in the word box than you will need.

eternal life	conscience	free will	sanctifying grace	charity	theological virtues
	natural law	sin	virtues	common good	morality	hope

1. _____ the grace that makes us holy, or one with God

2. _____ the power to choose to love and serve God and to choose to make him the center of our lives

3. _____ the reward of being a faithful disciple of Christ

4. _____ the foundation of the moral life for everyone, the original sense of right and wrong that is part of our very being that enables us to know by human reason good and evil

5. _____ what we knowingly and freely choose to do or say that sets us against God's love for us and turns our hearts away from that love

6. _____ the greatest of the virtues that enables us to love God simply because he is God and enables us to love our neighbors and ourselves because of our love for God

7. _____ the gift of God that is part of every human being that helps us judge right from wrong

8. _____ the virtue that helps us keep our eyes on the kingdom of heaven and enables us to trust in God and all his promises above all else

9. _____ spiritual powers or habits or behaviors that help us do what is right and avoid what is wrong

10. _____ the strengths or habits God gives us to help us attain holiness that are the pillars on which our life in Christ is built

Remembering Our Faith

TRUE OR FALSE. Write T next to the statements that are true. Write F next to the statements that are false.

11. _____ God has left us on our own to live our life in Christ.

12. _____ Every person is born with a well-formed conscience.

13. _____ The more we work at being happy, the more difficult it is to live a holy life.

14. _____ Our intention, or motive for choosing to do something, affects the goodness or evil of our action.

15. _____ All authority flows from God.

COMPLETE EACH SENTENCE. Insert the letter of the word or phrase that best completes each sentence.

16. The _____ is the spiritual part of the human person that never dies.

   a. intellect
   b. free will
   c. soul
   d. all of the above

17. _____ sin turns our hearts away from God.

   a. Mortal
   b. Venial
   c. Social
   d. All of the above

18. _____ is the greatest of the virtues.

   a. Faith
   b. Hope
   c. Love
   d. Wisdom

19. _____ is the moral virtue that gives us strength and courage to do the morally right thing.

   a. Prudence
   b. Justice
   c. Temperance
   d. Fortitude

20. _____ is the ability to choose to make God the center of our lives.

   a. Holiness
   b. Actual grace
   c. Free will
   d. Intellect

Understanding Our Faith

TELL WHAT YOU HAVE LEARNED IN THIS CHAPTER. Write a two-sentence reflection for each of these items.

21. Compare holiness and happiness.

_____

_____

_____

_____

22. Describe what Jesus asks of anyone who wishes to be his disciple.

_____

_____

_____

_____

23. Explain how the Christian moral life can be a path to freedom.

_____

_____

_____

_____

24. Describe how Christ has repaired our relationship with God.

_____

_____

_____

_____

Living Our Faith

WRITE A SHORT PARAGRAPH.

25. What are you doing or can you do to build a well-formed and well-informed conscience?

_____

_____

_____

_____

What I'll Remember

WRITE A SHORT PARAGRAPH.

Think back over all the new things you learned in Unit 1 of Morality. What did you find the most interesting? Tell why you remember it and explain what difference it will make in your life of faith.

_____

_____

_____

_____

Portfolio

WRITE A SHORT PARAGRAPH.

If you are creating a portfolio of your work in this class, think back over the items you added during this unit. Which one represents your best work? Describe it and tell what you learned by doing it.

_____

_____

_____

_____

Faith Vocabulary

MATCH FAITH TERMS WITH THEIR MEANINGS. In each space provided, write the term that best fits the definition. There are more terms in the word box than you will need.

Decalogue precept perjury presumption sacrifice idol reverence

1. _____ a word meaning "ten words," another term for the Ten Commandments

2. _____ false gods; whatever takes the place of God in our life

3. _____ the attitude of awe, profound respect, and love

4. _____ a rule or principle that imposes a standard of conduct or behavior on people

5. _____ taking of a false oath by calling on God to be a witness to a lie

Remembering Our Faith

COMPLETE EACH SENTENCE. Insert the letter of the word or phrase that best completes each sentence.

6. The taking of a false oath by calling on God to be a witness to a lie is called _____.
   a. blasphemy
   b. perjury
   c. simony
   d. atheism

7. The rejection or denial of the existence of God is called _____.
   a. sacrilege
   b. superstition
   c. atheism
   d. simony

8. To engage in _____ is to worship something or someone in place of God.
   a. atheism
   b. perjury
   c. idolatry
   d. none of the above

9. The abuse of spiritual power for personal gain is called _____.
   a. simony
   b. idolatry
   c. superstition
   d. both a and b

10. The mistreating of anyone or anything that is consecrated for worshiping God is called _____.
    a. idolatry
    b. simony
    c. sacrilege
    d. none of the above

TRUE OR FALSE. Write T next to the statements that are true. Write F next to the statements that are false.

11. _____ The Ten Commandments are God's gifts to all people.

12. _____ The teachings of Jesus replaced the Ten Commandments.

13. _____ The First Commandment asks us to make sure that God is somewhere on our list of priorities.

14. _____ For Christians Sunday is the Lord's Day, the day on which Jesus was born.

15. _____ The name *YHWH* was not spoken aloud by faithful Israelites.

Understanding Our Faith

TELL WHAT YOU HAVE LEARNED IN THIS CHAPTER. Write a two-sentence reflection for each of these items.

16. What is the connection between the Ten Commandments and the natural law?

_____

_____

17. What is the heart of the teaching of the First Commandment?

_____

_____

18. What is the heart of the teaching of the Second Commandment?

_____

_____

19. What is the heart of the teaching of the Third Commandment?

_____

_____

Living Our Faith

WRITE A SHORT PARAGRAPH. Use a separate piece of paper for your answer.

20. "Get your priorities straight" is an adage, or wise saying. How do the Ten Commandments guide you in following this adage?

Morality

Faith Vocabulary

MATCH FAITH TERMS WITH THEIR MEANINGS. In each space provided, write the term that best fits the definition. There are more terms in the word box than you will need.

Liturgy of the Hours   Hail Mary   confidence   Martha
intercession   disciple   petition   doubt   Mary

1. _____ a quality of discipleship

2. _____ a person who learns from another person and follows and spreads that person's teaching

3. _____ a form of prayer that asks God to give us the grace we need to live our daily lives

4. _____ the daily public prayer of the Church

5. _____ a form of prayer that asks God to bless, heal, and take care of the needs of others

Remembering Our Faith

COMPLETE EACH SENTENCE. Insert the letter of the word or phrase that best completes each sentence.

6. _____ was the brother of Martha and Mary.
   a. John
   b. Mark
   c. Lazarus
   d. Matthew

7. _____ was a disciple of Jesus who is a model of prayerful listening.
   a. Martha
   b. Mary
   c. Joanna
   d. None of the above

8. _____ is an example of an outgoing disciple who is a model for serving others.
   a. Martha
   b. Mary
   c. Joanna
   d. None of the above

9. True Christian discipleship involves _____.
   a. prayerful listening
   b. confidence
   c. faith
   d. all of the above

10. An attitude of _____ is NOT a quality of discipleship.
   a. faith and trust
   b. self-absorption
   c. confidence
   d. prayerful listening

TRUE OR FALSE. Write T next to the statements that are true. Write F next to the statements that are false.

11. _____ The Gospel shows us that Jesus traveled with his disciples.

12. _____ In Jesus' time it would have been out of the ordinary for Jesus to have spoken to and explained his teachings publicly to women.

13. _____ Luke's account of the Gospel is centered on Jesus' journey to and from Nazareth.

14. _____ Both prayer and serving others are part of true Christian discipleship.

15. _____ The foundation of Christian discipleship is listening to and learning from Jesus.

Understanding Our Faith

TELL WHAT YOU HAVE LEARNED IN THIS CHAPTER. Write a two-sentence reflection for each of these items.

16. What does the Gospel story of the widow of Nain teach us about being a disciple of Jesus?

   _____

   _____

17. What does the Gospel story about Jesus and the Samaritan woman at the well teach us about being a disciple of Jesus?

   _____

   _____

18. What does the story of Martha and Mary reaching out to Jesus when their brother dies teach us about discipleship?

   _____

   _____

19. Compare the role of prayer and service in the life of a disciple of Jesus.

   _____

   _____

Living Our Faith

WRITE A SHORT PARAGRAPH. Use a separate piece of paper for your answer.

20. How can prayerfully reading and thinking about the Scriptures help you live as a disciple of Jesus?

Faith Vocabulary

MATCH FAITH TERMS WITH THEIR MEANINGS. In each space provided, write the term that best fits the definition. There are more terms in the word box than you will need.

| obedience   war   suicide   capital punishment |
| Fourth Commandment   euthanasia   direct abortion |

1. _____ the intentional and direct killing of oneself

2. _____ the direct and intentional killing of an unborn child

3. _____ the respectful listening and trusting response to a person who has authority over us and is using their authority appropriately

4. _____ the lawful execution of people as punishment for certain crimes that the Catholic Church teaches should be rarely used

5. _____ the direct and intentional killing of a person who is suffering from a long-term or even terminal illness

Remembering Our Faith

COMPLETE EACH SENTENCE. Insert the letter of the word or phrase that best completes each sentence.

6. _____ are sins against the Fifth Commandment.
   a. Murder
   b. Direct abortion
   c. Euthanasia
   d. All of the above

7. The Fourth Commandment teaches that we are to show respect to _____.
   a. parents
   b. teachers
   c. people in legitimate authority
   d. all of the above

8. The Catholic Church teaches that all other means should be exhausted before resorting to _____.
   a. war
   b. capital punishment
   c. euthanasia
   d. both a and b

9. We honor and respect all life as sacred because _____.
   a. every human person is created in God's image and likeness
   b. God shares his life and love with every person
   c. God commands us to respect all human life
   d. all of the above

10. As citizens we respect legitimate civil authority by _____.
    a. working with them in a spirit of justice
    b. exercising our right to vote
    c. paying taxes
    d. all of the above

TRUE OR FALSE. Write T next to the statements that are true. Write F next to the statements that are false.

11. _____ The family is the heart and center of all other human communities.

12. _____ Christian parents have the responsibility to teach their children that the first calling of a Christian is to follow their parents.

13. _____ Christians have a responsibility to work to change sinful policies established by civic authorities.

14. _____ Every human life is equally sacred.

15. _____ The Catholic Church teaches that society should always utilize capital punishment for certain crimes.

Understanding Our Faith

TELL WHAT YOU HAVE LEARNED IN THIS CHAPTER. Write a two-sentence reflection for each of these items.

16. Compare obeying a parent with honoring a parent.

_____

_____

17. Describe how citizens and civil authorities can work together to build a just community.

_____

_____

18. Explain the Catholic Church's teaching on capital punishment.

_____

_____

19. Describe how abuse of alcohol and other drugs is related to respect for the sacredness of human life.

_____

_____

Living Our Faith

WRITE A SHORT PARAGRAPH. Use a separate piece of paper for your answer.

20. Describe some of the many ways young people are tempted to violate or disregard the sacredness of human life. How might Catholic teenagers stand up against that violence?

Faith Vocabulary

MATCH FAITH TERMS WITH THEIR MEANINGS. In each space provided, write the term that best fits the definition. There are more terms in the word box than you will need.

chastity sexuality modesty discrimination temperance
stewardship reparation

1. _____ the returning or replacing of another person's goods that we have unjustly taken or damaged

2. _____ the virtue that guides us in living out our relationships with other people with patience and moderation.

3. _____ the virtue that guides us in expressing our sexuality properly according to our state in life

4. _____ the gift through which we express and share our life and love most intimately with and for others

5. _____ the managing of and caring for the property of another person or other people

Remembering Our Faith

COMPLETE EACH SENTENCE. Insert the letter of the word or phrase that best completes each sentence.

6. _____ is gravely contrary to the teachings of the Sixth Commandment.

   a. Adultery
   b. Fornication
   c. Sex before marriage
   d. All of the above

7. Stealing is the unjust taking of another person's _____ .

   a. possessions
   b. knowledge
   c. self-respect
   d. all of the above

8. Discrimination in employment is a form of theft and is contrary to the _____.

   a. Sixth Commandment
   b. Seventh Commandment
   c. Ninth Commandment
   d. none of the above

9. The Seventh Commandment guides us in dealing with our concerns for _____.

   a. the future
   b. people who are poor
   c. the common good
   d. all of the above

TRUE OR FALSE. Write T next to the statements that are true. Write F next to the statements that are false.

10. _____ Sensuality is the gift of being a man or a woman.

11. _____ According to God's plan of creation, the only proper place for intimate sexual activity is in marriage.

12. _____ Everyone is obliged to live a chaste life.

13. _____ All of creation belongs first of all to God the Creator.

14. _____ The Church has a preferential love for people who are oppressed by poverty.

15. _____ The making of a profit is always evil.

Understanding Our Faith

TELL WHAT YOU HAVE LEARNED IN THIS CHAPTER. Write a two-sentence reflection for each of these items.

16. Describe the relationship between the Sixth and Ninth Commandments.

   _____

   _____

17. Summarize the teaching of the Seventh Commandment.

   _____

   _____

18. Explain how the virtue of temperance helps us live the Sixth Commandment.

   _____

   _____

19. Compare the responsibilities of the employee with those of the employer.

   _____

   _____

Living Our Faith

WRITE A SHORT PARAGRAPH. Use a separate piece of paper for your answer.

20. In what ways can you live responsibly as a steward of God's creation?

Faith Vocabulary

MATCH FAITH TERMS WITH THEIR MEANINGS. In each space provided, write the term that best fits the definition. There are more terms in the word box than you will need.

lying	perjury	covet	rash judgment	avarice	greed	envy

1. _____ an excessive passion for wealth and the power that is often connected with wealth

2. _____ the capital sin of being saddened by the blessings other people have

3. _____ intentionally deceiving another person by deliberately saying what is false

4. _____ to wrongfully desire the blessings of another person

5. _____ the unchecked desire to have more and more things

Remembering Our Faith

COMPLETE EACH SENTENCE. Insert the letter of the word or phrase that best completes each sentence.

6. Rash judgments, detraction and calumny all injure the _____ or good name of a person.

    a. reputation
    b. heart
    c. soul
    d. none of the above

7. To say one thing and mean another is _____.

    a. perjury
    b. duplicity
    c. boasting
    d. none of the above

8. To act like we do not care or disguise our true feelings is _____.

    a. duplicity
    b. dissimulation
    c. boasting
    d. none of the above

9. When we pretend to be something we are not or believe in something we do not really believe in we engage in _____.

    a. collusion
    b. dishonor
    c. hypocrisy
    d. perjury

TRUE OR FALSE. Write T next to the statements that are true. Write F next to the statements that are false.

10. _____ A good reputation and honor are part of every person's dignity.

11. _____ All our blessings are signs of generosity of God toward all people.

12. _____ Justice demands that we repair the damage or harm caused by our acts against the truth.

13. _____ When we honor and respect the blessings of other people, we are showing our honor and respect for God too.

14. _____ A person who lives the virtue of detachment has no use for possessions.

15. _____ The Ninth Commandment teaches that we are to be people of our word.

Understanding Our Faith

TELL WHAT YOU HAVE LEARNED IN THIS CHAPTER. Write a two-sentence reflection for each of these items.

16. What is the heart of the teaching of the Eight Commandment?

_____

_____

17. What is the heart of the teaching of the Tenth Commandment?

_____

_____

18. How can those who work in the electronic media violate the Eighth Commandment?

_____

_____

19. Describe a person who lives the virtue of detachment.

_____

_____

Living Our Faith

WRITE A SHORT PARAGRAPH. Use a separate piece of paper for your answer.

20. The Gospel teaches that when we say yes, we are to mean yes (see Matthew 5:37). How can that Gospel teaching guide you in living as a follower of Jesus?

Faith Vocabulary

MATCH FAITH TERMS WITH THEIR MEANINGS. In each space provided, write the term that best fits the definition. There are more terms in the word box than you will need.

Lord's Prayer	temptation	kingdom of God	trespass
hallowed	daily bread	petitions	Glory Prayer

1. _____ all that tries to move us away from living holy lives

2. _____ the prayer that Jesus taught his disciples

3. _____ a word that means goodness and holiness

4. _____ the heart of Jesus' preaching

5. _____ phrase that includes our spiritual and material needs

Remembering Our Faith

COMPLETE EACH SENTENCE. Insert the letter of the word or phrase that best completes each sentence.

6. In Matthew's Gospel Jesus taught his disciples the Our Father _____.

   a. at the Last Supper
   b. in the synagogue at Nazareth
   c. in the Sermon on the Mount
   d. in the Temple in Jerusalem

7. The second half of the Our Father acknowledges _____.

   a. our dependence on God
   b. God cares for us
   c. our forgiveness must have no limits
   d. all of the above

8. The phrase "hallowed be thy name" in the Our Father refers to the _____ of God.

   a. Fatherhood
   b. holiness
   c. forgiveness
   d. none of the above

9. The phrase "daily bread" in the Our Father refers to our _____ needs.

   a. spiritual
   b. material
   c. both a and b
   d. none of the above

TRUE OR FALSE. Write T next to the statements that are true. Write F next to the statements that are false.

10. _____ Jesus taught the disciples the Our Father at the Last Supper.

11. _____ The first half of the Our Father describes the Christian belief in God and his plan for us.

12. _____ In the Our Father we express our hope in eternal life with God.

13. _____ At the heart of Jesus' preaching is the announcement of the coming of the kingdom of God.

14. _____ In the Our Father we affirm that God has a plan for all creation.

15. _____ In the Our Father we acknowledge that we sometimes turn our heart away from God's love.

Understanding Our Faith

TELL WHAT YOU HAVE LEARNED IN THIS CHAPTER. Write a two-sentence reflection for each of these items.

16. Explain what it means to call God our Father.

_____

_____

17. Describe how it is possible for people to do God's will.

_____

_____

18. Describe how we are called to forgive those who hurt us.

_____

_____

19. Describe the Lord's Prayer as a model for Christian living.

_____

_____

Living Our Faith

WRITE A SHORT PARAGRAPH. Use a separate piece of paper for your answer.

20. How can praying the Lord's Prayer guide you in living as a follower of Jesus?

Morality

Faith Vocabulary

MATCH FAITH TERMS WITH THEIR MEANINGS. In each space provided, write the term that best fits the definition. There are more terms in the word box than you will need.

precept	greed	idol	chastity	sexuality	reparation	euthanasia
	disciple	avarice	natural law	envy	avarice	

1. _____ anything or anyone that takes the place of God in our life

2. _____ a rule or principle that imposes a standard of conduct or behavior on people

3. _____ the foundation of all human laws engraved on the human heart

4. _____ the returning or replacing of another person's goods that we have unjustly taken or damaged

5. _____ an excessive passion for wealth and the power that can accompany wealth

6. _____ the virtue that guides us in expressing our sexuality according to our state in life

7. _____ the direct and intentional killing of a person who is suffering from a long-term or even terminal illness

8. _____ the gift of being a man or a woman, a boy or a girl

9. _____ the capital sin of being saddened by the blessings other people have

10. _____ the unchecked desire to have more and more

Remembering Our Faith

TRUE OR FALSE. Write T next to the statements that are true. Write F next to the statements that are false.

11. _____ Jesus fulfilled the revelations of the old Law.

12. _____ Jesus replaced the Ten Commandments and told his disciples to live the Beatitudes in place of the Ten Commandments.

13. _____ Every human life, even the life of a person who commits a horrifying crime, is sacred.

14. _____ Every person has the responsibility and the obligation to live a chaste life.

15. _____ We are obliged to reveal the truth to everyone—no exceptions.

COMPLETE EACH SENTENCE. Insert the letter of the word or phrase that best completes each sentence.

16. _____ is the taking of a false oath by calling on God to witness to a lie.

   a. Idolatry
   b. Sacrilege
   c. Perjury
   d. Atheism

17. _____ is the mistreating of anyone or anything that is set apart, or consecrated, for worshiping God.

   a. Idolatry
   b. Sacrilege
   c. Perjury
   d. Simony

18. _____ is the direct and intentional killing of a child conceived but not yet born.

   a. Euthanasia
   b. Direct abortion
   c. Suicide
   d. all of the above

19. _____ is gravely contrary to the teachings of the Sixth Commandment.

   a. Adultery
   b. Sex before marriage
   c. Fornication
   d. All of the above

20. Stealing is the unjust taking of another person's _____ .

   a. possessions
   b. knowledge
   c. self-respect
   d. all of the above